I Am A Woman.
I Am a Treasure!

I Am Covered!
31-Day Declarations And Devotional Prompters For Security and Satisfaction

Written and Designed By Damola Treasure Okenla

Published By

HILLTOP
Creative Publishers
PUSHING OUT THE MESSAGE FROM WITHIN

Strength and dignity are her clothing and her position is strong and secure; she rejoices over the future [the latter day or time to come, knowing that she and her family are in readiness for it]!

Proverbs 31:25

THIS IS A GIFT

FROM :

TO :

CONTENTS

INTRODUCTION

To be covered means to be protected and be secured from all manners of attacks, harassment and troubles of life.

To be covered means
- To Protect
- To Shield
- To Shelter
- To Enclose

To be spiritually covered is to have supernatural insurance with God(Psalm 37:3-4)

As a treasured woman, the daughter of the Most High God, adversity is not your final destination and should not be your destruction (Romans 8:38 -39)

You are under cover of God by the
- Word of God (Colossians 3:16; Romans 10:8; Psalm 119:11)
- The Blood of Jesus (Exodus 12:13; Colossians 1:20; Romans 5:9;Hebrews 2:14; 12:24;13:21; Revelations 12:11;Isaiah 53:5; Galatians 3:13; Zechariah 9:11
- The name of Jesus
- The love of God (1 John 3:10; John 3:16;1 John 4:19; John 14:15; John 13: 34 - 35; I John 4: 18; Romans 12:9;5:5; Ephesians 3:18 -20,19)
- Fellowship of the brethren(1 Corinthians 10:1,5 ; 1 Thessalonians 5:11; Hebresw10:25; Ecclesiates 4:9-12; proverbs 27:17)
- God's protective armor (Ephesians 6 :10 -18;4:14; 6:12; 1 Peter 5:8;James 4:7; 2 Corinthians 10:4-5)
- God's rest (Hebrews 4:9 ; John 14:15; Hebrews 4:1-3; Matthew 11:28 -30; Romans 10:17; Isaiah 1:19; Phillipians 4:6-7; 1 Peter 5:7; Romans 15 :13)

First off, you have to be born again into the family of God, so that you indeed be under the cover (Psalm 91)

That is why there is an assurance that no matter what you are going through or what your situation is, God will arise for you. You Are Covered!

INTRODUCTION

SALVATION PRAYER
Dear Heavenly Father

 I come to you in the name of Jesus Christ.

Your Word says, " But everyone my Father has given to me, they will come. And all who come to me, I will embrace, and I will never turn them away." (John 6:37), so I know You will not cast me away, but you embrace me, and I am grateful for that.

You said in Your Word, " Everyone who calls on the name of the LORD will be rescued and experience new life." (Romans 10:13). I am calling on Your name, so I know I am saved now and entered into a new life.

You said, " For if you publicly declare with your mouth that Jesus is LORD and believe in your heart that God raised from the dead, you will experience salvation (Romans 10:9-10). I believe in my heart Jesus Christ is the Son of God. I believe that He was raised from the dead for my justification, and I confess Him now as my LORD.

Father, Your Word says, " With the heart, man believes unto righteousness," and I do believe with my heart, I have now become the righteousness of God in Christ (2 Corinthians 5:21), And I am saved.

Thank You, LORD !

Name :
Signed:
Date:

God loves His daughters and cares for them throughout the ages.

God cares for women and expressly speaks for them when it matters.

Jesus called women's daughter and healed them.

Jesus was not ashamed of interacting with women in public.

God turned women otherwise messy stories to eternal divine messages.

Women were protected and rescued from accusations and condemnations.

God called women good.

You are a woman . You are a Treasure. Strength and dignity are your clothing. Your position is strong and secure. Your future is bright, beautiful and blessed. Rejoice!

JESUS IN DEFENCE
OF A WOMAN

JOHN 8:1-11

THE WOMAN CAUGHT IN
ADULTERY

She was accused but got a fair
judgment from Jesus.

Jesus walked up the Mount of Olives[a] near the city where he spent
the night.

Then at dawn Jesus appeared in the temple courts again, and soon
all the people gathered around to listen to his words, so he sat down
and taught them.

Then in the middle of his teaching, the religious scholars[b] and the
Pharisees broke through the crowd and brought a woman who had
been caught in the act of committing adultery and made her
stand in the middle of everyone.

Then they said to Jesus, "Teacher, we caught this woman in the very
act of adultery.

Doesn't Moses' law command us to stone to death a woman like
this? Tell us, what do you say we should do with her?"

They were only testing Jesus because they hoped to trap him with
his own words and accuse him of breaking the laws of Moses.But
Jesus didn't answer them. Instead he simply bent down and wrote in
the dust with his finger.

Angry, they kept insisting that he answer their question, so Jesus
stood up and looked at them and said,

"Let's have the man who has never had a sinful desire[f] throw the
first stone at her." And then he bent over again and wrote some
more words in the dust.

Upon hearing that, her accusers slowly left the crowd one at a time,
beginning with the oldest to the youngest, with a convicted
conscience.

Until finally, Jesus was left alone with the woman still standing
there in front of him. So he stood back up and said to her, "Dear
woman, where are your accusers? Is there no one here to condemn
you?"

Looking around, she replied, "I see no one, Lord."Jesus said, "Then I
certainly[j] don't condemn you either. Go, and from now on, be free
from a life of sin."

8

JESUS DELIVERED A WOMAN FROM EVIL CYCLE OF MARITAL PATTERNS AND FAILURE

JOHN 4

THE WOMAN BY THE WELL

Jesus arrived at the Samaritan village of Sychar, near the field that Jacob had given to his son, Joseph, long ago. Wearied by his long journey, he sat on the edge of Jacob's well. He sent his disciples into the village to buy food, for it was already afternoon.Soon a Samaritan woman came to draw water. Jesus said to her, "Give me a drink of water." Surprised, she said, "Why would a Jewish man ask a Samaritan woman for a drink of water?"

Jesus replied, "If you only knew who I am and the gift that God wants to give you—you'd ask me for a drink, and I would give to you living water."

The woman replied, "But sir,[you don't even have a bucket and this well is very deep. So where do you find this 'living water'?

Do you really think that you are greater than our ancestor Jacob who dug this well and drank from it himself, along with his children and livestock?"

Jesus answered, "If you drink from Jacob's well you'll be thirsty again and again,

but if anyone drinks the living water I give them, they will never thirst again and will be forever satisfied! For when you drink the water I give you it becomes a gushing fountain of the Holy Spirit, springing up and flooding you with endless life!"

9

GOD DEFENCE OF WOMEN

JOHN 4:1 -23

THE WOMAN BY THE WELL

The woman replied, "Let me drink that water so I'll never be thirsty again and won't have to come back here to draw water."

Jesus said, "Go get your husband and bring him back here."

"But I'm not married," the woman answered."That's true," Jesus said,

"for you've been married five times[g] and now you're living with a man who is not your husband. You have told the truth."

The woman said, "You must be a prophet!

So tell me this: Why do our fathers worship God here on this nearby mountain, but your people teach that Jerusalem is the place where we must worship. Which is right?"Jesus responded,

"Believe me, dear woman, the time has come when you won't worship[j] the Father on a mountain nor in Jerusalem, but in your heart.

Your people don't really know the One they worship. We Jews worship out of our experience, for it's from the Jews that salvation is made available.

GOD DEFENCE OF WOMEN

JOHN 4

THE WOMAN BY THE WELL

From here on, worshiping the Father will not be a matter of the right place but with the right heart. For God is a Spirit, and he longs to have sincere worshipers who worship and adore him in the realm of the Spirit and in truth."

The woman said, "This is all so confusing, but I do know that the Anointed One is coming—the true Messiah. And when he comes, he will tell us everything we need to know."

Jesus said to her, "You don't have to wait any longer, the Anointed One is here speaking with you—I am the One you're looking for."

At that moment the disciples returned and were stunned to see Jesus speaking with the Samaritan woman. Yet none of them dared to ask him why or what they were discussing.

All at once, the woman dropped her water jar and ran off to her village and told everyone.

"Come and meet a man at the well who told me everything I've ever done!

He could be the Anointed One we've been waiting for." Hearing this, the people came streaming out of the village to go see Jesus.

JESUS STOOD UP FOR A WOMAN CRITICISED FOR DOING GOOD

MATTEHW 26:6 -13

THE WOMAN WHO ANOINTED JESUS

She wa accused and criticized for doing good, and for some of us, we have faced the same issue, criticized for doing good. We get attack by people who which to do that which we do but are not able. In that case, you don't have to feel bad. God sees like He saw that woman, and He would shut the mouth of your critics.

Then Jesus went to Bethany, to the home of Simon, a man Jesus had healed of leprosy. A woman came into the house, holding an alabaster flask filled with fragrant and expensive oil. She walked right up to Jesus, and in a lavish gesture of devotion, she poured out the costly oil, and it cascaded over his head as he was at the table. When the disciples saw this, they were offended. "What a total waste!" they grumbled.
"We could have sold it for a great deal of money and given it to the poor."
Jesus knew their thoughts and said to them, "Why are you critical of this woman? She has done a beautiful act of kindness for me.
You will always have someone poor whom you can help, but you will not always have me.
When she poured the fragrant oil over me, she was preparing my body for burial.
I promise you that as this wonderful gospel spreads all over the world, the story of her lavish devotion to me will also be mentioned in memory of her."

GOD SUPERNATURALLY MET THE NEED OF A REJECTED AND LONELY WOMAN

GENESIS 16

HAGAR' S STORY

Now Sarai, Abram's wife, had not been able to bear children for him. But she had an Egyptian servant named Hagar. So Sarai said to Abram, "The Lord has prevented me from having children.
Go and sleep with my servant. Perhaps I can have children through her." And Abram agreed with Sarai's proposal.
So Sarai, Abram's wife, took Hagar the Egyptian servant and gave her to Abram as a wife. (This happened ten years after Abram had settled in the land of Canaan.)
So Abram had sexual relations with Hagar, and she became pregnant. But when Hagar knew she was pregnant, she began to treat her mistress, Sarai, with contempt.
Then Sarai said to Abram, "This is all your fault! I put my servant into your arms, but now that she's pregnant she treats me with contempt. The Lord will show who's wrong—you or me!" Abram replied, "Look, she is your servant, so deal with her as you see fit." Then Sarai treated Hagar so harshly that she finally ran away.

GOD SUPERNATURALLY MET THE NEED OF A REJECTED AND LONELY WOMAN

GENESIS 16

HAGAR' S STORY

The angel of the Lord found Hagar beside a spring of water in the wilderness, along the road to Shur.
The angel said to her, "Hagar, Sarai's servant, w
here have you come from, and where are you going?"
"I'm running away from my mistress, Sarai," she replied.
The angel of the Lord said to her, "Return to your mistress, and submit to her authority."
Then he added, "I will give you more descendants than you can count."
And the angel also said, "You are now pregnant and will give birth to a son. You are to name him Ishmael (which means 'God hears'), for the Lord has heard your cry of distress.
This son of yours will be a wild man, as untamed as a wild donkey! He will raise his fist against everyone, and everyone will be against him. Yes, he will live in open hostility against all his relatives."
Thereafter, Hagar used another name to refer to the Lord, who had spoken to her. She said, "You are the God who sees me."
She also said, "Have I truly seen the One who sees me?"
So that well was named Beer-lahai-roi (which means "well of the Living One who sees me"). It can still be found between Kadesh and Bered.
So Hagar gave Abram a son, and Abram named him Ishmael. Abram was eighty-six years old when Ishmael was born.

GOD SUPERNATURALLY MET THE NEED OF A REJECTED AND LONELY WOMAN

GENESIS 21:10 -20

HAGAR'S STORY :ANOTHER ENCOUNTER

So she turned to Abraham and demanded, "Get rid of that slave woman and her son. He is not going to share the inheritance with my son, Isaac. I won't have it!"

This upset Abraham very much because Ishmael was his son. But God told Abraham, "Do not be upset over the boy and your servant. Do whatever Sarah tells you, for Isaac is the son through whom your descendants will be counted.

But I will also make a nation of the descendants of Hagar's son because he is your son, too." So Abraham got up early the next morning, prepared food and a container of water, and strapped them on Hagar's shoulders.

Then he sent her away with their son, and she wandered aimlessly in the wilderness of Beersheba. When the water was gone, she put the boy in the shade of a bush. Then she went and sat down by herself about a hundred yards away. "I don't want to watch the boy die," she said, as she burst into tears.

But God heard the boy crying, and the angel of God called to Hagar from heaven, "Hagar, what's wrong? Do not be afraid! God has heard the boy crying as he lies there. Go to him and comfort him, for I will make a great nation from his descendants." Then God opened Hagar's eyes, and she saw a well full of water. She quickly filled her water container and gave the boy a drink. And God was with the boy as he grew up in the wilderness. He became a skillful archer,.

15

JESUS HEALED A WOMAN

LUKE 13:10 -13

THE STORY OF THE CRIPPLED WOMAN

One Sabbath day, while Jesus was teaching in the synagogue, he encountered a seriously handicapped woman. She was crippled and had been doubled over for eighteen years. Her condition was caused by a demonic spirit of bondage that had left her unable to stand up straight.

When Jesus saw her condition, he called her over and gently laid his hands on her. Then he said, "Dear woman, you are free. I release you forever from this crippling spirit." Instantly she stood straight and tall and overflowed with glorious praise to God!

JESUS HEALED THE WOMAN WHO WAS SICK FOR TWELVE YEARS

MARK 5:25-34

THE STORY OF THE WOMAN WITH THE ISSUE OF BLOOD

Now, in the crowd that day was a woman who had suffered horribly from continual bleeding for twelve years.[a] 26 She had endured a great deal under the care of various doctors, yet in spite of spending all she had on their treatments, she was not getting better, but worse. When she heard about Jesus' healing power, she pushed through the crowd and came up from behind him and touched his prayer shawl. For she kept saying to herself, "If only I could touch his clothes, I know I will be healed." As soon as her hand touched him, her bleeding immediately stopped! She knew it, for she could feel her body instantly being healed of her disease! Jesus knew at once that someone had touched him, for he felt the power that always surged around him[d] had passed through him for someone to be healed. He turned and spoke to the crowd, saying, "Who touched my clothes?" His disciples answered, "What do you mean, who touched you? Look at this huge crowd—they're all pressing up against you." But Jesus' eyes swept across the crowd, looking for the one who had touched him for healing. When the woman who experienced this miracle realized what had happened to her, she came before him, trembling with fear, and threw herself down at his feet, saying, "I was the one who touched you." And she told him her story of what had just happened. Then Jesus said to her, "Daughter, because you dared to believe, your faith has healed you. Go with peace in your heart, and be free from your suffering!"

GOD STOOD UP FOR THE WOMEN WHO DEMANDED FOR WHAT WAS RIGHTFULLY THEIRS. STOOD AGAINST GENDER DISCRIMINATION AND BECAME PACESETTERS.

NUMBERS 27:1-11

THE STORY OF THE DAUGHTERS OF ZELOPHEHAD

One day a petition was presented by the daughters of Zelophehad— Mahlah, Noah, Hoglah, Milcah, and Tirzah. Their father, Zelophehad, was a descendant of Hepher son of Gilead, son of Makir, son of Manasseh, son of Joseph. These women stood before Moses, Eleazar the priest, the tribal leaders, and the entire community at the entrance of the Tabernacle. "Our father died in the wilderness," they said. "He was not among Korah's followers, who rebelled against the Lord; he died because of his own sin. But he had no sons. Why should the name of our father disappear from his clan just because he had no sons? Give us property along with the rest of our relatives. So Moses brought their case before the Lord. And the Lord replied to Moses, "The claim of the daughters of Zelophehad is legitimate. You must give them a grant of land along with their father's relatives. Assign them the property that would have been given to their father. "And give the following instructions to the people of Israel: If a man dies and has no son, then give his inheritance to his daughters. And if he has no daughter either, transfer his inheritance to his brothers. If he has no brothers, give his inheritance to his father's brothers. But if his father has no brothers, give his inheritance to the nearest relative in his clan. This is a legal requirement for the people of Israel, just as the Lord commanded Moses."

GOD COMPESATED A WOMAN WHO UNLOVED BECAUSE OF HER LOOK

GENESIS 29:31-35

THE LEAH STORY

When the Lord saw that Leah was unloved, he enabled her to have children, but Rachel could not conceive.

So Leah became pregnant and gave birth to a son. She named him Reuben, for she said, "The Lord has noticed my misery, and now my husband will love me.

She soon became pregnant again and gave birth to another son. She named him Simeon, for she said, "The Lord heard that I was unloved and has given me another son."

Then she became pregnant a third time and gave birth to another son. He was named Levi, for she said, "Surely this time my husband will feel affection for me, since I have given him three sons!"

Once again Leah became pregnant and gave birth to another son. She named him Judah, for she said, "Now I will praise the Lord!" And then she stopped having children.

COVERAGE FOR THE TREASURED WOMAN

AUTHORITY OVER THE ENEMY

Revelations 12:11; James 4:7;1 John 1:7;John 8:31-32;Luke 24:49; 2 Timothy 1:5 ; Mark 16:17; Romans 8:37; 1 Peter 5:8-9; Ephesians 6:16; 1 John 4:1; 2 Corinthians 10: 3-5; Romans 16:20

SPIRITUAL STRENGTH

Ephesians 6:10; Psalm 27:1; 46:1;119:28; Genesis 18:14; Philippians 4:13; Isaiah 40:29 31; Colossians 1:11-12; Ephesians 3:16 ; Habakkuk 3:19

TRUSTING GOD

Proverbs 3:5-6; Psalms 7:1; 34:8; 37:3-4,5-7; Hebrews 10:23; Romans 10:17; Proverbs 2:1; 4:20-22; 112:7

WHOLENESS AND HEALING

Colossians 2:9-10; , 6,7; 1:9-20; Revelations 1:11 ; Psalm 103:1 -3 ; Marks 7:27 ; Exodus 15 :26; Isaiah 53 : 5 ; Matthew 8:17; Jeremiah 30 :16 +17

GOD'S PROVISION

Phillipians 4 : 19 ; Lamentations 3:23; Phillipians 4 :19; Matthew 6 : 31 - 33 ; Psalm 37 : 4 ; Psalm 23 ; 2 Corinthians 9:8 ; Job 36 :11 ;1 Chronicles 29 :11; Proverbs 8:18 ; 1 Kings 17 : 8 -24 ; 2 Kings 4 : 1 - 7

COVERAGE FOR THE TREASURED WOMAN

ABUSE

Isaiah 53:5-6; Psalm 22:7-8.16;Zephniah 3:17;Psalm 142:1-7;59:1;
31:4;61:3; 62:7 ;140:1-6; 61:1-4; Isaiah 43:18-19;Phillipians 3:13;
Matthew 10:26; Psalm 103:3-11; 1 Thessalonians 1:6-7; Hebrews
4:16;Phillipians 4:6-7;2 Corinthians 12:9-10;Psalm 17:8-9; 46; Isaiah
25:4; Revelations 21 :1-4

ANXIETY & WORRY

Job 23:8-9; Psalm 73:2-3;142:4;Phillipians 4:8;Proverbs 12:25 Jobs 6:1-3;
1 Peter 4:6-7; Isaiah 41:10; 2 Corinthians 12:9-10; Phillipians 4:13,19;
Psalms 139:16;Isaiah 26:3-4; Matthew 6:33-34; John 14:1-3; Jeremiah
32:24-27

DISPPOINTMENT/BROKEN HEART

Psalm 56:8; Isaiah 61:1; Job 23:8-10; Proverbs 19:21; Isaiah 25:1;
Jeremiah 29:11-13; James 1:2-5; Galatians 6:2; Romans 15:1-2 ; 1 Peter
5:7-9; Psalm 34:18;147:3; Ecclesiates 3:11;John 14:1,27; 2 Corinthians 1
: 3 -4

LONELINESS

Psalm 102 :7 -11 ; 38 :9-11; Job 19 :13 -14; Psalm 142 1-4 ; Job 23 : 8 -9 ;
Psalm 13 :1 ; 25 :16; 143 : 8 -10 ; 62 :5-8; Deuteronomy 31:6 ; Joshua 1:9
; Hebrews 13:5 ; John 16 :32 ; Zephaniah 3:17 ; Psalm 68 :5 -6; Psalm 73
: 25 -26

COVERAGE FOR THE TREASURED WOMAN

SELF - WORTH

Genesis 1: 26 -27 ; John 3: 16; Ephesians 2 : 4 -7 ; 1 John 4:10 ;
Ephesians 1:4 - 6 ; 1 Peter 1 : 18 -20 ; Jeremiah 31:3 ; Ephesians 2:10 ; 1
Peter 2 :9 ; Ephesians 1 : 17 -19 ; 17 -20 ; Phillipians 3 : 8 -9 ; Jeremiah 9
:23 -24 ; Psalm 10 : 4 ; 2 Corinthians 10 :12;Deuteronmy 26: 18 ; 1
Corinthians 7:23 ; Psalm 119:37; Luke 10 :42; Acts 20 : 24

COMFORT IN DISTRESS

Romans 8:26; Psalm 10: 17 ; 94:19 ; 119 : 50 - 52 , 76 ; 2 Thessalonians.
2 : 16 - 17 ; Job 42 : 11 ; 21 : 2 ; Ruth 2 :13 ; 1 Corinthians 14 :3 ; 2
Thessalonians 2 :16 -17 ; Jonah 2 : 1-2 ; Psalm 130 : 1 -2 ; 57:1 ; 25; 25;
34; 37; 40; 28;54 ; Jonah 1+3; Ruth 1 - 4

GUIDANCE

Psalm 32: 8; 25: 4, 9 ; 23 ; Exodus 33: 13; Numbers 10:31 ; Romans 8:14
; Proverbs 3 : 5 -7 ; Psalms 37 : 23 ; 43 :3 ; 48: 14; 143 : 8 ;

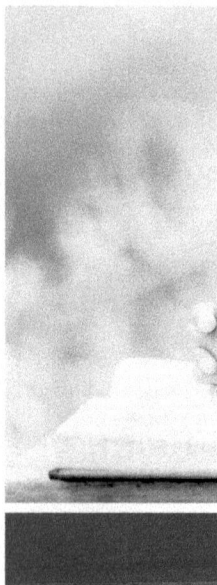

SCRIPTURES

Live under the protection of God Most High and stay in the shadow of God All-Powerful. Then you will say to the Lord,"You are my fortress, my place of safety; you are my God, and I trust you." The Lord will keep you safe from secret traps and deadly diseases (Psalm 91:1-3)

Offer praise to God our Savior because of our Lord Jesus Christ! Only God can keep you from falling and make you pure and joyful in his glorious presence. Before time began and now and forevermore, God is worthy of glory, honor, power, and authority. Amen (Jude 1:24-25

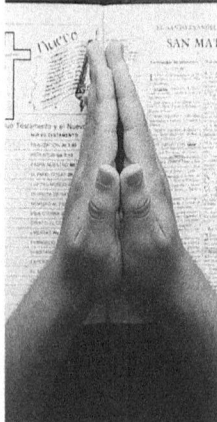

The Lord gives perfect peace to those whose faith is firm. So always trust the Lord because he is forever our mighty rock (Isaiah 26:4-5)

I'm covered. God is my refuge, my fortress, and my place of safety. I'm hidden in His strength.

GOD IS THE MIGHTY ROCK. THE ROCK OF AGES. THE ROCK ETERNAL.

REFLECTION
In what or whom do you place your safety and security?

#DECLAREIT 2

I am covered!
I have placed all my
trust in the Lord, so I
have the assurance
that I cannot be
defeated. I'm
unshakeable and
unmoveable by
anything or anybody.

**YOUR SAFETY AND
SECURITY ARE ROOTED
DEEPLY IN GOD'S
PRESENCE.**

REFLECTION
Wisdom is seeking
more of God's
presence. Meditate
on Psalm 63:1-2

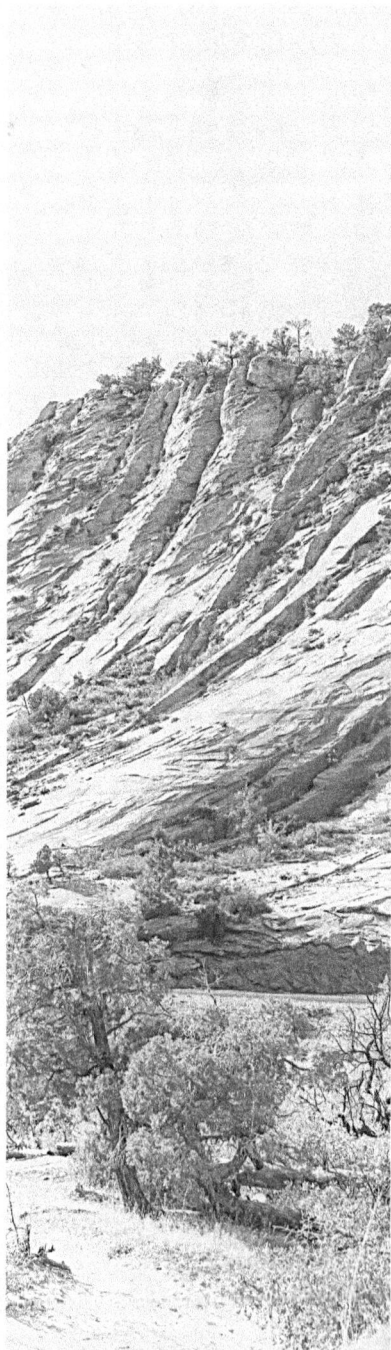

25

I am covered!
God, the Jehovah
Yahweh is my shield.
He surrounds me with
Himself and covers me
continually

WORSHIP GOD AS JEHOVAH-SHAMMAH. THE OMNIPRESENT GOD! ASK HIM TO MANIFEST HIS PRESENCE IN YOUR SITUATION.

REFLECTION
Ponder over Genesis
28:18. What does it mean
to you?

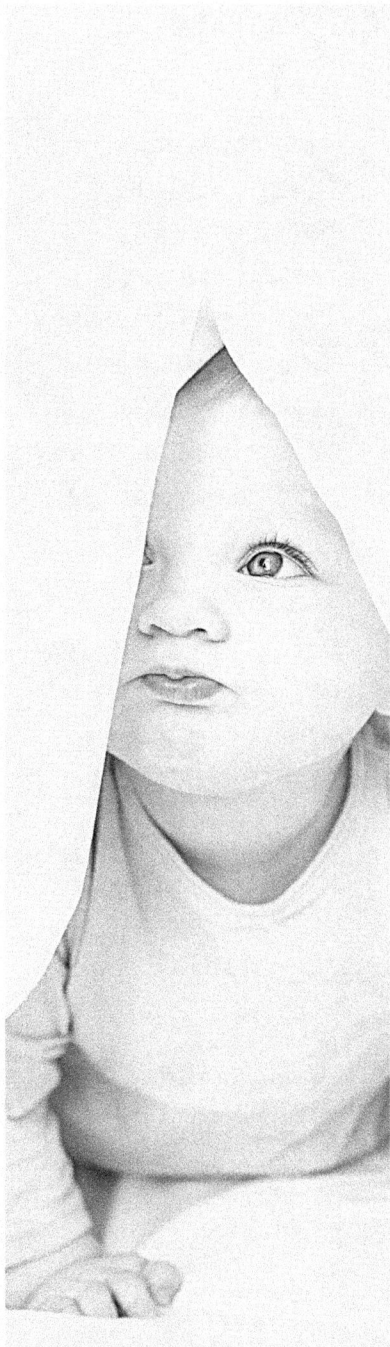

26

I am covered!
I fear nothing
because God is
always ready to
help me. His strong
and powerful hand
is holding me
securely against any
manner of trouble.

**GOD IS THE
SHELTER FOR THE
OPPRESSED AND A
REFUGE IN TIMES
OF TROUBLE.**

REFLECTION
Are you in any
trouble? Consider
responding to the
invitation of Jesus in
Matthew 11:28 -29

#DECLAREIT 5

I am covered!
I am secured in God's faithfulness. Great is His faithfulness towards me and mine.

IN A WORLD FULL OF UNCERTAINTIES, WE NEED AN ANCHOR SUCH AS THE CONSTANCY OF GOD'S FAITHFULNESS.

REFLECTION
Ask God to help you to be faithful in your love to Him in response to His faithfulness to you
(LAM.3:22-23)

SCRIPTURES

But in the depths of my heart I truly know that you, Yahweh, have become my Shield;You take me and surround me with yourself. Your glory covers me continually.]You lift high my head when I bow low in shame (PS.3:3)

All who are oppressed may come to you as a shelter in the time of trouble, a perfect hiding place. May everyone who knows your mercykeep putting their trust in you,for they can count on you for help no matter what.O Lord, you will never, no never, neglect thosewho come to you (PS.9:9-10)

Confidence and strength flood the hearts of the lovers of God who live in awe of him,and their devotion provides their children with a place of shelter and security (PRO.14:26})
With passion I pursue and cling to you.Because I feel your grip on my life,I keep my soul close to your heart (PS.63 :8)

#DECLAREIT 6

I am covered!
I am shielded from
harm. No evil shall
prevail against me. No
disease shall infect me.
No disaster shall come
near me.

**LIVING WITHIN THE
SHADOW OF GOD
MOST HIGH IS THE
SECRET PLACE, NOT
BY MERE
RECITATION.
_PSALM 91**

REFLECTION
Ensure you wear
your shield of faith
at every moment
(EPH.6:16)

#DECLAREIT 7

I am covered!
God can turn my tragedy
to triumph. His grace is
sufficient in any
adverse circumstance.

"WHEN WE ARE IN A
SITUATION WHERE
JESUS IS ALL WE
HAVE, WE SOON
DISCOVER HE IS ALL
WE NEED." _ GIGI
GRAHAM TCHIVIDJAN

REFLECTION
Ask God to help you learn
lessons in good and bad
times. And to be able to
share the experiences
with others.

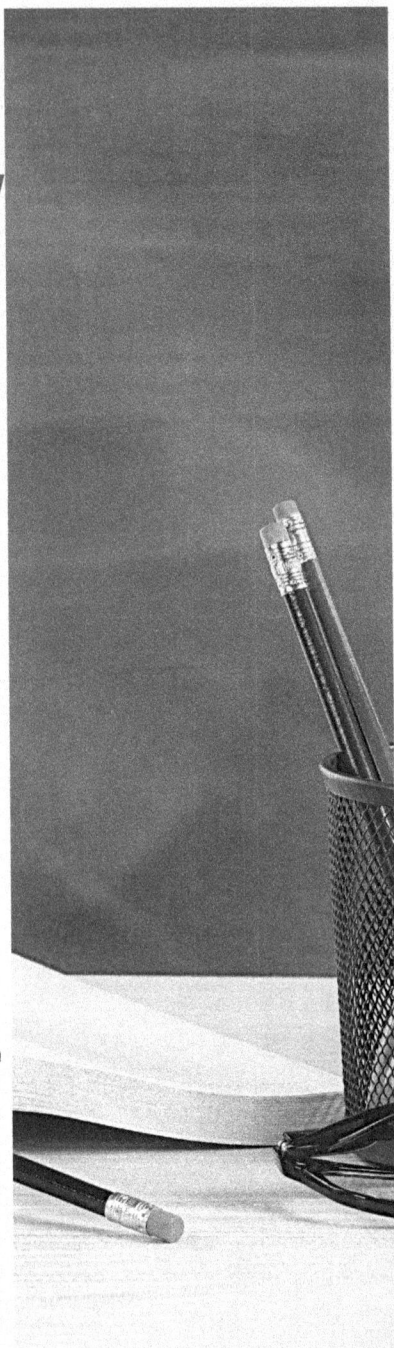

#DECLAREIT 8

I am covered!
I am anointed for
my journey in
destiny. No one is
permitted to touch
me for evil
regardless of status
and position in
society.

**GOD HAS THE POWER
TO BUILD OR REMOVE
THE HEDGE AROUND A
PERSON.**

REFLECTION
Pray against breaking
the HEDGE OF God
around you (Ecc. 10:8;
Job 1; PS.125:1-3

#DECLAREIT 9

I am covered!
No scheme or
weapon of
destruction that
could work against
me has been forged.
God is my defense
and will always
grant me victory.

**NOT THAT THE
ENEMY WILL NOT
TRY BUT SHALL
NOT FINALLY
PREVAIL OVER
YOU. -JEREMIAH
1: 18-19; PSALMS
11:2**

REFLECTION
Sing: In Christ Alone.

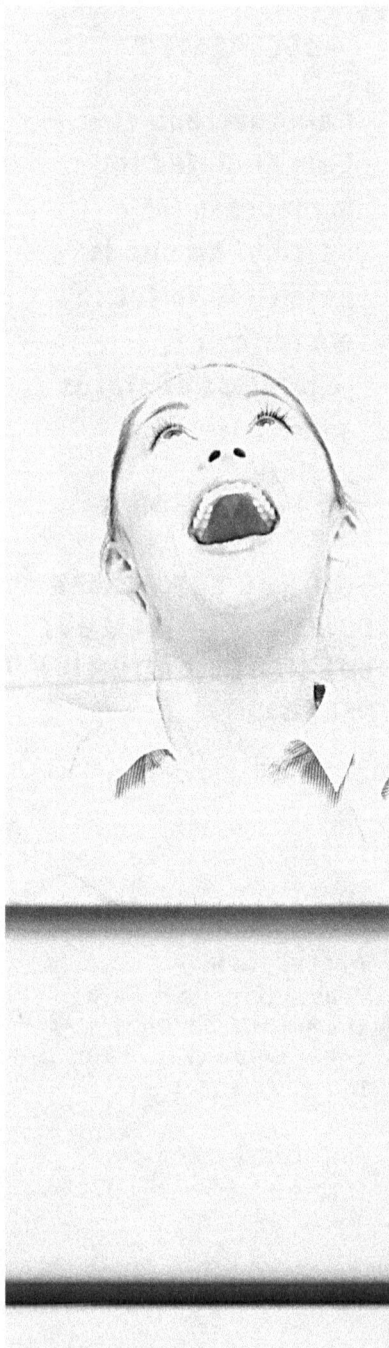

#DECLAREIT 10

I am covered!
I am getting the
best of care; The
LORD is my good
shepherd, I lack
nothing beneficial.

GOD CARES
ABOUT
EVERYTHING
ABOUT US-
EVERY LITTLE
THING. HE
NUMBERED THE
HAIRS OF OUR
HEAD (LUKE
12:7)

REFLECTION
Ask Him for your
need (Phil.4: 6,19;
Ps.145:14-16 ;MT.7:7)

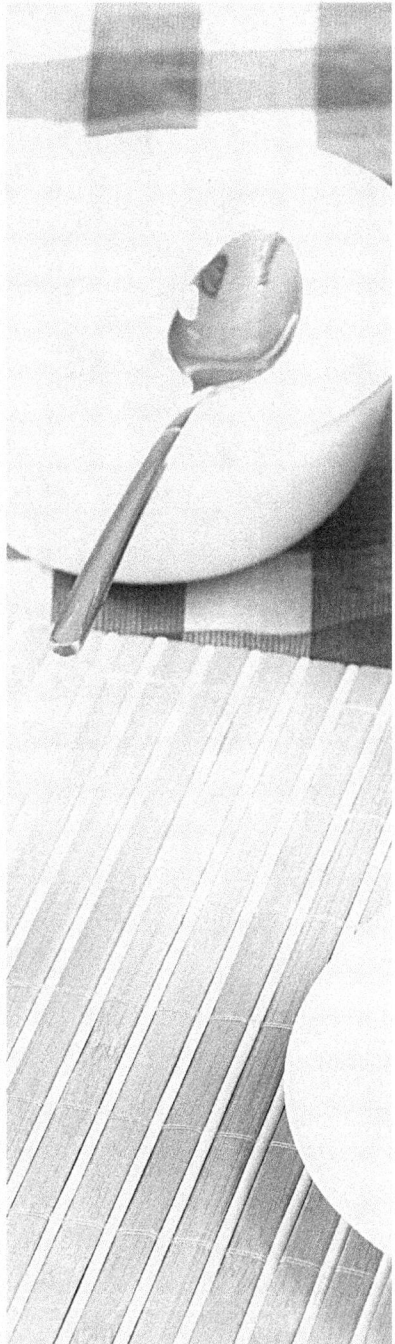

"

Through many dangers, toils, and snares, I have already come; 'Tis grace has brought me safe thus far, And grace will lead me home.

JOHN NEWTON

SCRIPTURES

The faithful love of the Lord never ends! His mercies never cease.23 Great is his faithfulness;   his mercies begin afresh each morning (LAM.3:22-23)

When we live our lives within the shadow of God Most High,our secret hiding place, we will always be shielded from harm.How then could evil prevail against us or disease infect us? (PS.91:9-10)

Please, God, show me mercy!Open your grace-fountain for me,for you are my soul's true shelter.I will hide beneath the shadow of your embrace,under the wings of your cherubim,until this terrible trouble is past(PS.57:1)

The character of God is a tower of strength,[a]for the lovers of God delight to run into his heartand be exalted on high (PRO.18:10)

I am covered!
I have the
assurance of
deliverance from
all my fears,
distress, and
troubles.

**GOD IS THE
MIGHTY AND
ABLE
DELIVERER.**

REFLECTION
Worship God as the
DELIVERER- PSALM
107; 34; Daniel 3;6;1
COR. 15:57

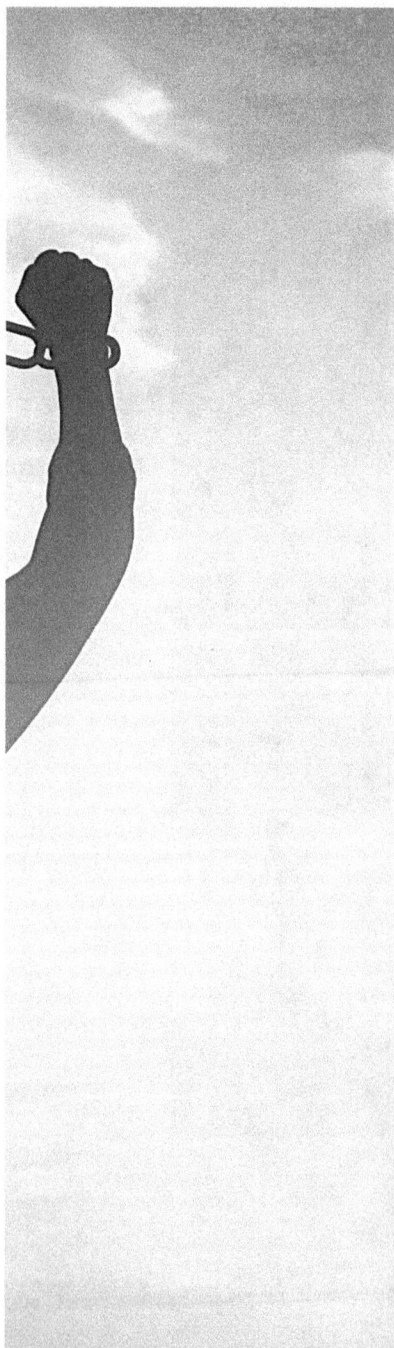

I am covered!
I have the
confidence that I
shall not be a victim
to the wickedness of
the wicked. The rod
of the wicked rising
up against me and
mine is broken, in
Jesus' name.

"THE WICKED ALWAYS
CRAVE WHAT IS EVIL;
THEY ' LL SHOW NO
MERCY AND GET NO
MERCY." -PRO.21:10

REFLECTION
Ask God to search your
heart for any trace of
wickedness; ask for
mercy and cleansing
(PS.139: 23 -24)

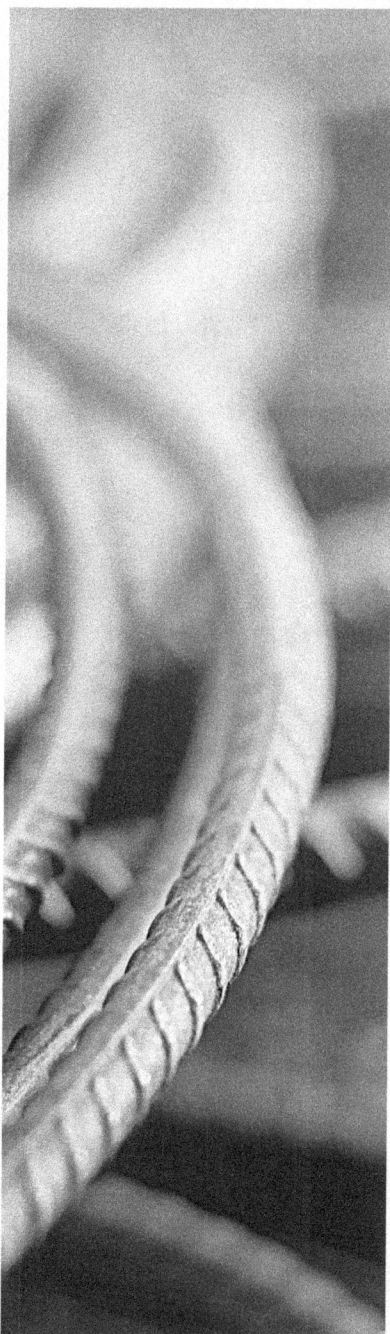

I am covered!
I cannot be
intimidated by
anything or
anybody. No force
shall be able to
stand before me
all the days of my
life.

DON'T CONSENT TO
OTHERS DARKEN
YOUR LIGHT BECAUSE
IT'S SHINING
BRIGHTER THAN
THEIRS.

_ DAMOLA TREASURE
OKENLA

REFLECTION
READ FURTHER:
Joshua 1:1-9; 2 Timothy
1:7;Isaiah 41:10-
13;Deuteronomy 31:6

I am covered!
I have the
assurance of
healings and
divine
health.I'm
well and
whole,
nothing
missing or
lacking!

"FOR I AM THE
LORD WHO HEALS
YOU." _ GOD
OUR GOD IS
JEHOVAH -
ROPHI.

REFLECTION
Ps. 103: 1-5;107:19-20;
PRO.4:20 -23; ISA.58: 6-
11; JER. 30: 16 -17;
MAL.4:2-3; MT7:7-11;
ACTS 10:38

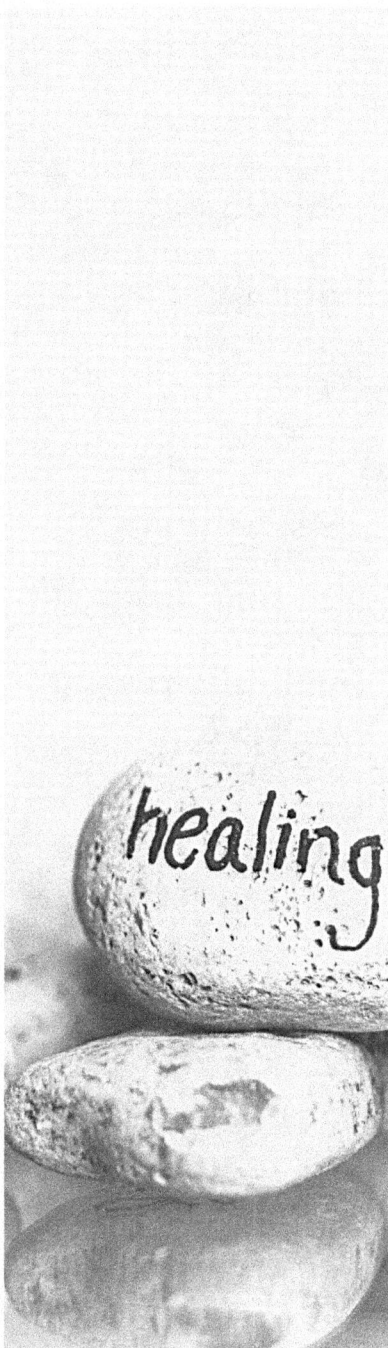

40

#DECLAREIT 15

I am covered! God is fighting my battles while I remain still and silent; No fear, no fretting.

"FAITH.WITHOUT TROUBLE OR FIGHTING, IS A SUSPICIOUS FAITH; FOR TRUE FAITH IS A FIGHTING, WRESTLING FAITH."
_ RALPH ERSKINE

REFLECTION
Hand that battle over to God.
PS. 46:10; 37:7;131:2; ISA.30:15;EX. 14:14

66

The safest place in all the world is in the will of God, and the safest protection in all the world is the name of God.

WARREN WIERSBE

SCRIPTURES

Little children, you can be certain that you belong to God and have conquered them, for the One who is living in you is far greater than the one who is in the world (1 JN. 4:4

I sought the Lord, and He heard me,And delivered me from all my fears (PS.34:4)

The righteous cry out,
and the Lord hears,And delivers them out of all their troubles (PS. 34:17

)Then they cried out to the Lord in their trouble,And He delivered them out of their distresses (PS. 107:6)

I am convinced that my God will fully satisfy every need you have, for I have seen the abundant riches of glory revealed to me through the Anointed One, Jesus Christ!

Philippians 4:19 TPT

#DECLAREIT 16

I am covered!
My God, the LORD
Himself, is with
me. He will not fail
me or abandon me.
I am, therefore,
determined and
confident.

**GOD IS FOREVER
FAITHFUL AND CAN
BE TRUSTED.**

REFLECTION
Worship God as the
DELIVERER- PSALM 107;
34; Daniel 3;6; 1 COR.
15:57

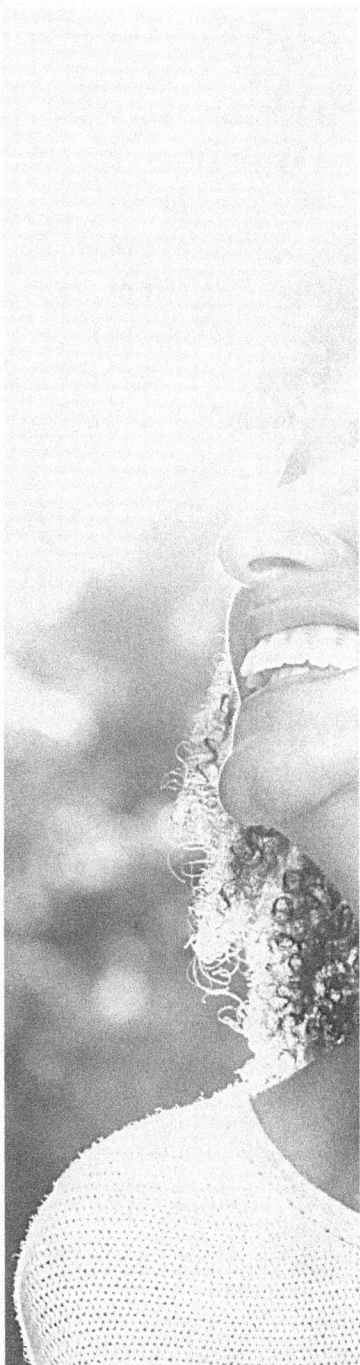

I am covered!
The spiritual
weapons at my
disposal are more
than sufficient to
help me against
battle visible or
invisible. I'm not
losing at all!

OUR SPIRITUAL
WEAPONS ARE
ENERGIZED WITH
DIVINE POWER TO
DISMANTLE THE
DEFENCES BY PEOPLE
HIDE EFFECTIVELY.

REFLECTION
Do you know you're the
spiritual weapons at
your disposal?
Eph. 6:12-18; 2 Cor.10:4-6

#DECLAREIT 18

I am covered!
I don't have to
employ humans'
weapons of
manipulation to
achieve my
purpose. All I need
is to align myself
with God's plans for
me.

" I ALONE KNOW THE
PLANS I HAVE FOR
YOU, PLANS TO BRING
YOU PROSPERITY AND
NOT DISASTER, PLANS
TO BRING ABOUT THE
FUTURE YOU HOPE
FOR."-GOD

REFLECTION
Whose plans are you
following in the
journey of destiny?

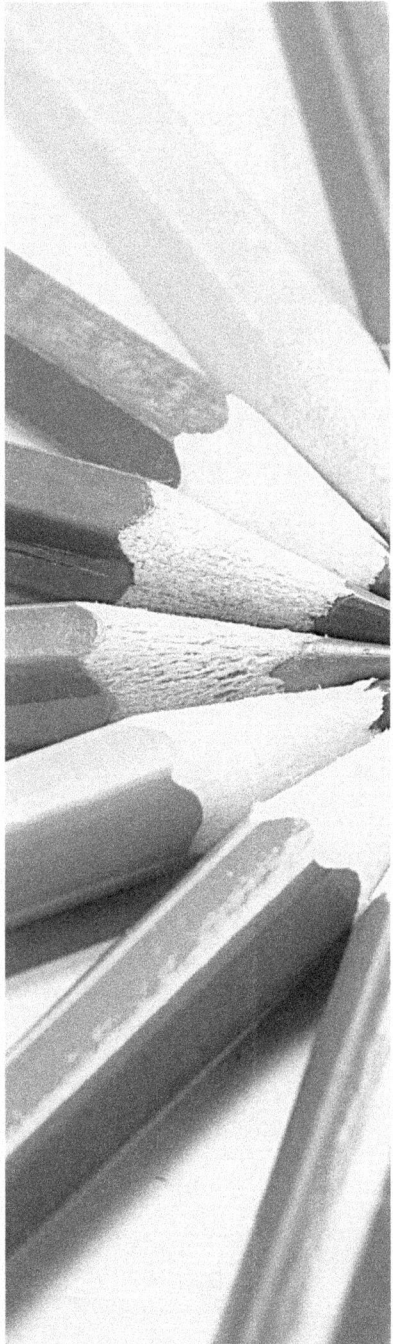

46

I'm covered
with the
assurance of
divine
presence. I
shall be rightly
guided and
preserved for
my purpose.

**GOD'S PRESENCE IS WHAT
MAKES THE DIFFERENCE.**

REFLECTION

THE VISION FOR YOUR LIFE
INVOLVES ASKING GOD FOR NEW
DIRECTIONS. YOUR STEPS WILL
CREATE BEAUTIFUL PATTERNS AS
YOU WALK IN HIS PRESENCE (ISA.
30:21; PS.32:8; JOSH.1:5,9)

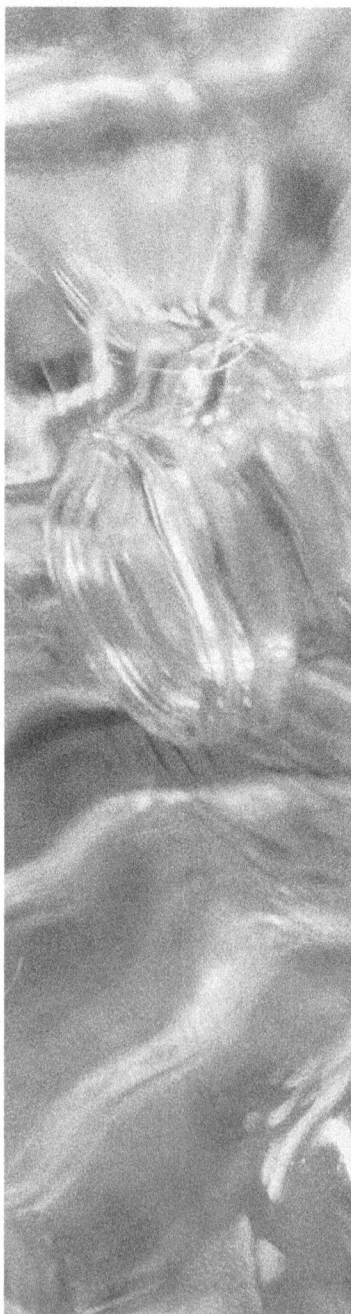

I'm covered with
the assurance of
divine protection
I put on the
whole armor of
God that I am
may be able to
stand against the
wiles of the
devil.

**GOD'S PROTECTION IS
WHAT KEEP YOU SAFE.
YOU DO NOT HAVE TO
ENGAGE IN SPIRITUAL
WARFARE IN YOUR
FLESH. GOD'S ARMOR
IS IMPENETRABLE.**

REFLECTION
PONDER OVER- EPH. 6:10-
18;4:14;1PET.5:8;JAMES
4:7;2 COR.10:4-5

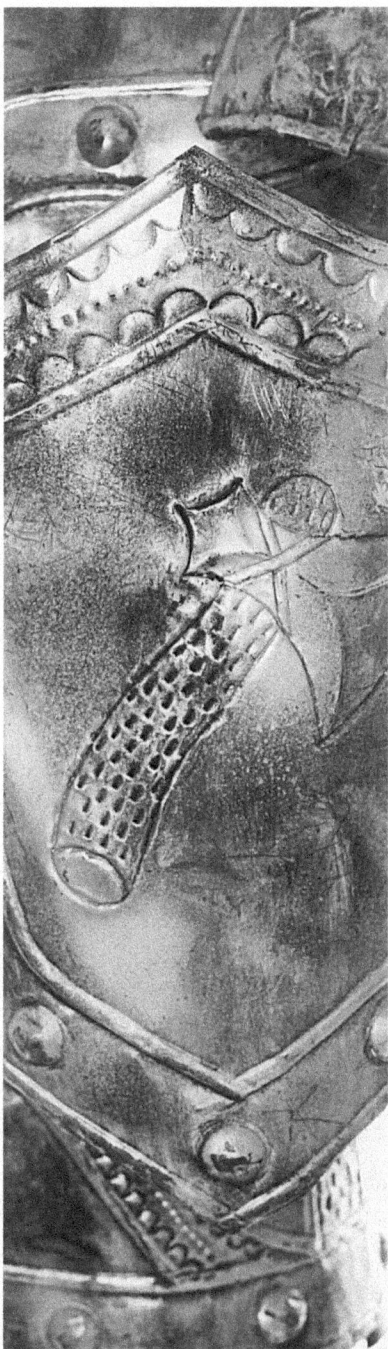

66

God's angels often protect his servants from potential enemies.

-BILLY GRAHAM

SCRIPTURES

In pride and arrogance the wicked hotly pursue and persecute the afflicted;Let them be caught in the plots which they have devised (PS.10:2)

They carry a mouthful of hexes,   their tongues spit venom like adders.They hide behind ordinary people,   then pounce on their victims.9 They mark the luckless,   then wait like a hunter in a blind;When the poor wretch wanders too close,   they stab him in the back.10-11 The hapless fool is kicked to the ground,   the unlucky victim is brutally axed.He thinks God has dumped him,   he's sure that God is indifferent to his plight (PS. 10: 8-11)

For you, God, will see to it that every pit-digger who works to trap and harm others will be trapped and harmed by his own treachery (PS. 7:16)

)He will not ignore forever all the needs of the poor,for those in need shall not always be crushed.Their hopes shall be fulfilled, for God sees it all! (PS.9:18)

#DECLAREIT 21

I'm covered with the assurance of divine preservation. I am untouchable by power, principality, or personality. My father forbids it.

YET GOD WOULD NOT PERMIT ANYONE TO TOUCH THEM, PUNISHING EVEN KINGS WHO CAME AGAINST THEM. HE SAID TO THEM, "DON'T YOU DARE LAY A HAND ON MY ANOINTED ONES, AND DON'T DO A THING TO HURT MY PROPHETS!" PSALMS 105:14-15 TPT

Ponder on John 8:1-11 and 2 Samuel 24:14; What does it tell you about the judgment of God versus the wisdom of men?

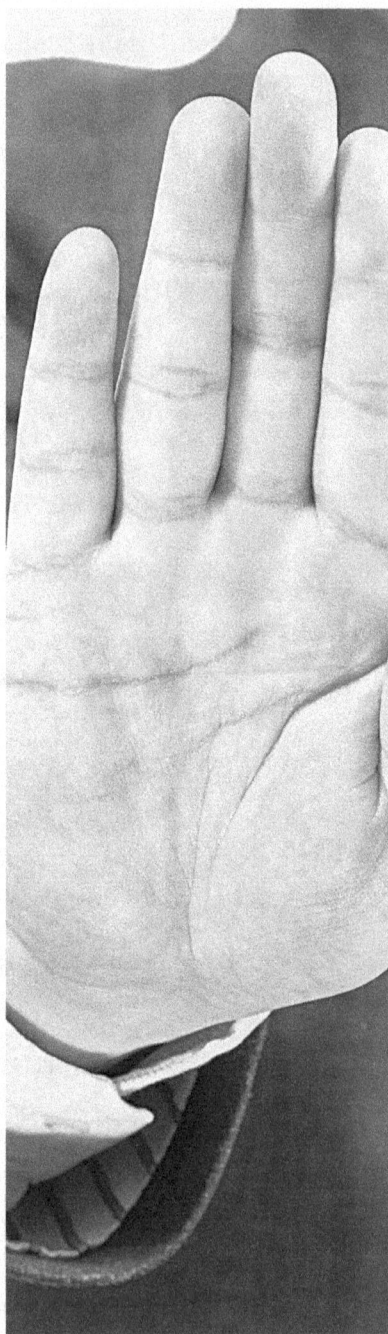

#DECLAREIT 22

I'm covered with the assurance of safety from all hidden dangers in every sphere and form - false accusations and any deadly curse. Every snare holding me back is broken, and I have escaped.

UNSEEN DANGERS AND TRAPS ARE LURKING AROUND TO DESTROY THROUGH DIVERSE KIND OF RELATIONSHIPS.

REFLECTION
PRAY FERVENTLY BEFORE YOU ENTER INTO ANY RELATIONSHIP OR PARTNERSHIP.

#DECLAREIT 23

I'm covered and strengthened to resist every contrary power. No matter how fierce the opposition against me, I am more than a conqueror!

SOME OPPOSITIONS ARE NOT BAD FOR US. THEY ARE CATALYST TO OUR NEXT LEVEL AND ADVANCEMENT.

REFLECTION
GOD'S PLAN AND PEOPLE' OPPOSITION ARE SOMETIMES INTERTWINED. GEN.39. 28-31; PS.105:16-25

#DECLAREIT 24

I'm covered to
become all that
God has ordained
me to become.
Nothing can stop
me, not my gender
or status.

THERE IS NO GREATER DISCOVERY THAN SEEING GOD AS THE AUTHOR OF YOUR DESTINY.

- RAVI ZACHARIAS

REFLECTION
AS YOU PONDER OVER
THESE SCRIPTURES. WHAT
DO THINK ABOUT YOUR
DESTINY?ISA.46:10;55:11;
JER.1:5;29:11; NUM.23:19;
PS.138:8; PRO.20:24

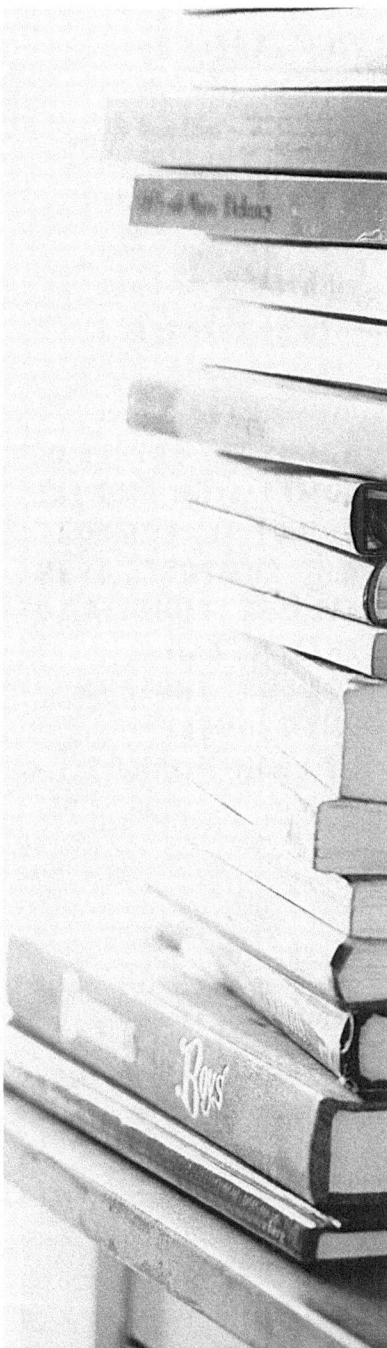

#DECLAREIT 25

I'm covered! It
does not matter
the difficulty I
am going
through or have
to go through.

GOD IS THE FATHER OF
COMPASSION AND THE
GOD OF ALL COMFORT
WHO COMFORTS US IN
ALL OUR TROUBLES,SO
THAT WE CAN
COMFORT THOSE IN
ANY TROUBLE.
- 2 CORINTHIANS 1:3-4

REFLECTION
DONT WASTE YOUR PAIN;
REPURPOSE IT FOR
SOMEONE'S GAIN.
CAN YOU FEEL GOD IN
YOUR SITUATION?

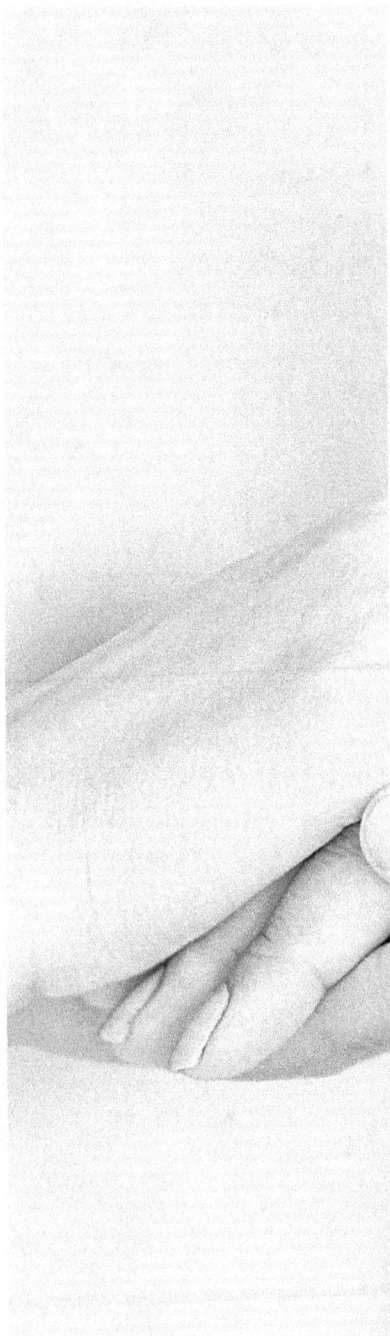

66

A God wise enough to create me and the world I live in is wise enough to watch out for me.

-PHILLIP YANCEY

SCRIPTURES

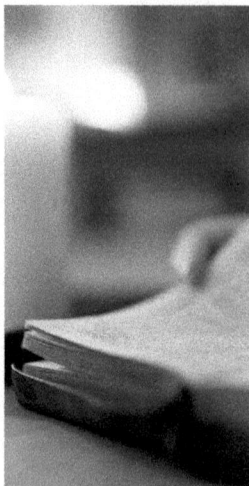

I patiently waited, Lord,   for you to hear my prayer.You listened and pulled me from a lonely pit   full of mud and mire.You let me stand on a rock   with my feet firm (PS..40: 1-2)

Those who trust in the Lord are as unshakeable , as unmovable as mighty Mount Zion! Just as the mountains surround Jerusalem,so the Lord's wrap-around presence surrounds his people, protecting them now and forever (PS.125:1-2)

But the one who always listens to me will live undisturbed in a heavenly peace.Free from fear, confident and courageous,you will rest unafraid and sheltered from the storms of life (PRO.1:33)

#DECLAREIT 26

I am covered! I Have placed all my trust In the Lord, so I have the assurance that I cannot be defeated. I am unshakable and unmoveable by anything or anybody.

TRUSTING HIM TO WORK OUT YOUR CIRCUMSTANCES INSTEAD OF USING YOUR OWN MIGHT AND POWER WILL BRING DEEP SATISFYING JOY INTO YOUR LIFE – JOYCE MEYERS

REFLECTION
MEDITATE ON THESE SCRIPTURES - PSALMS 25:3,20-21; ROMANS 8:31-39

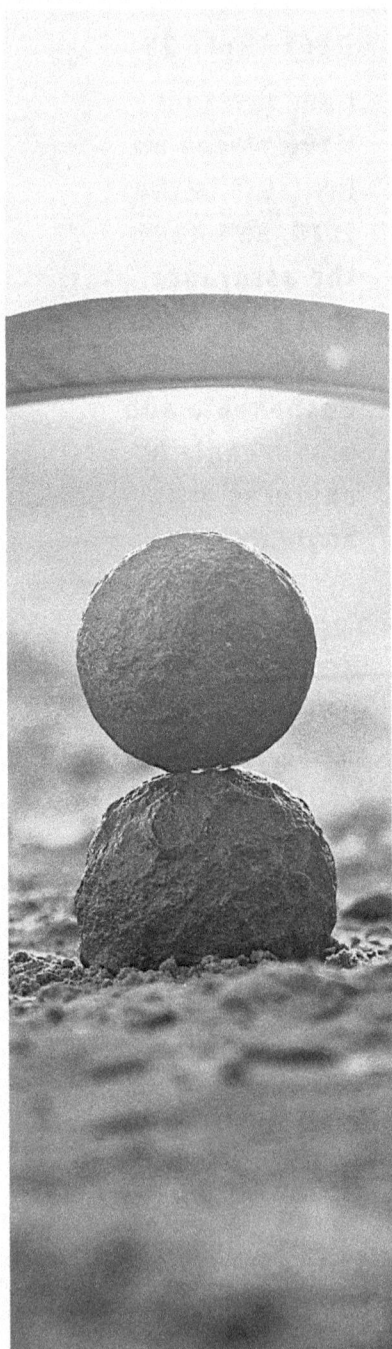

I am covered! God is with me all the days of my life. He promises never to leave me or forsake me. Even if I can not sense His presence at the moment, I still have the assurance that God is with me. He knows what I am going through, and He cares.

THE CHRISTIAN LIFE IS NOT A CONSTANT HIGH. I HAVE MY MOMENTS OF DEEP DISCOURAGEMENT. I HAVE TO GO TO GOD IN PRAYER WITH TEARS IN MY EYES AND SAY, 'O GOD, FORGIVE ME,' OR 'HELP ME.
-BILLY GRAHAM

REFLECTION

JOSHUA 1:1-9

#DECLAREIT 28

I am covered! The fact that I'm going through does not mean I'm forgotten. God has a plan for me, and He is working it out. Everything happening to me is not outside of His plan but part of the process.

FAITH...INVOLVES TRUSTING IN THE FUTURE PROMISES OF GOD AND WAITING FOR THEIR FULFILLMENT.

- R. C. SPROUL

REFLECTION
LEAN ON GOD. CALL ON GOD. TRUST GOD
READ
PROVERBS 3:5-7 IN DIFFERENT VERSION. MEDITATE ON IT.

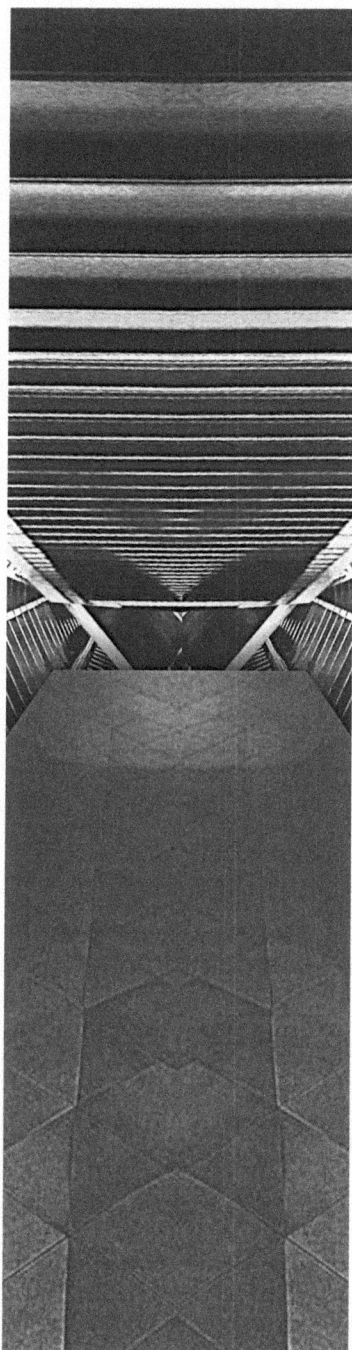

#DECLAREIT 29

I am covered! God is the pillar that holds my life. On Him, I can pour all my pains, fears, problems, burdens insecurities, shame, and anxieties. I receive comfort, strength, and encouragement.

Pour out all your worries and stress upon him and leave them there, for he always tenderly cares for you.
-1PETER 5:7

REFLECTION
God is WILLING TO HELP YOU. ALL YOU NEED TO DO IS TO RUN TO HIM.

#DECLAREIT 30

I am covered!
I will be still
and silent,
waiting on
Him to act for
me.

LEARNING HOW TO BE STILL, TO REALLY BE STILL AND LET LIFE HAPPEN - THAT STILLNESS BECOMES A RADIANCE.
MORGAN FREEMAN

REFLECTION
To be still takes time, and it means waiting on God. It's time to chill out, keep your mind at rest and listen to God' a whispers.PSALM 46:10

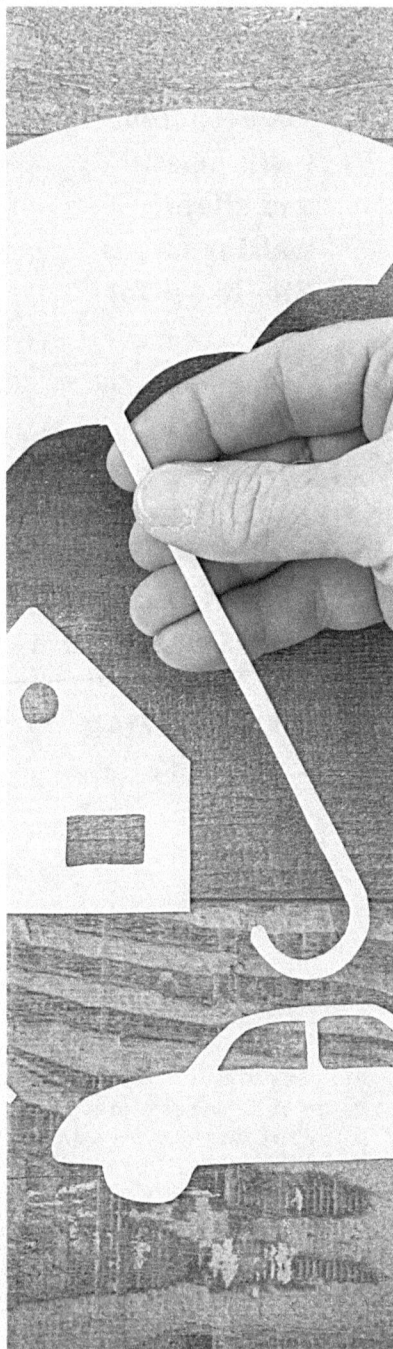

I am covered!
And my
coverage is
comprehensive.

PERSONS OF GODLY
CHARACTER ARE
NEITHER OPTIMISTS
NOR PESSIMISTS ,
BUT REALIIST WHO
HAVE CONFIDENCE IN
GOD.
WARREN WIERSBE

REFLECTION
Surrender all to God.
Galatians 2 :20; James 4:7;
Jeremiah 10 :23 ; Matthew
11 :28 ; Psalm 50 ; Romans
12: 1-2

66

The ultimate measure of a man is not where he stands in moments of comfort and convenience, but where he stands at times of challenge and controversy.

-MARTIN LUTHER KING JR.

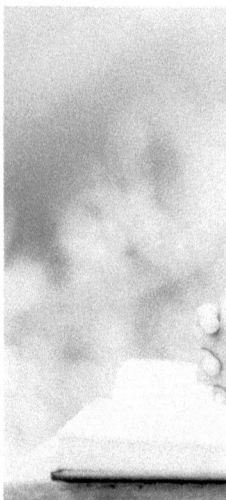

SCRIPTURES

Live under the protection of God Most High and stay in the shadow of God All-Powerful. Then you will say to the Lord,"You are my fortress, my place of safety; you are my God, and I trust you." The Lord will keep you safe from secret traps and deadly diseases (Psalm 91:1-3)

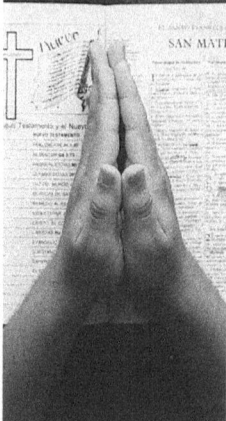

Offer praise to God our Savior because of our Lord Jesus Christ! Only God can keep you from falling and make you pure and joyful in his glorious presence. Before time began and now and forevermore, God is worthy of glory, honor, power, and authority. Amen (Jude 1:24-25

The Lord gives perfect peace to those whose faith is firm. So always trust the Lord because he is forever our mighty rock (Isaiah 26:4-5)

Be determined and confident. Do not be afraid of them. Your God, the Lord himself, will be with you. He will not fail you or abandon you."

Deuteronomy 31:6 GNT

PRAYER STARTERS

- Father, I worship You. You are my strength, and from You, I have my strength. You are my helper and my refuge. I declare You are worthy! Thank You for upholding me and not allowing me to stumble. You are my guardian who never dozes or sleep. You are right at my side to protect me, shielding me, and sheltering me. You guard me against every evil; you guard my very life. You guard me when I leave and when I return, You guard me before, and presently, You guard me always. Thank You, my guardian God, for answered prayers. Praise is awaiting You! (Psalm 91; 121; 1 Chronicles 4:9-10).

- Father, You are a merciful God, please have mercy on me for any way I have broken the hedge to allow the enemy into my life or environment. Search me O Lord and see and see my heart; test me and know my anxious thoughts. Point out anything in me that offends You and lead me along the path of everlasting life. By Your mercy, I recover every good ground I have lost to the enemy due to carelessness or ignorance. I close every broken hedge with the blood of Jesus. (Ecclesiastes 10:8; Psalm 139:23 -24).

- Father, let Your hands of power and favor prevail upon my destiny and divine calling. Provide me with Your protection, don't let evil hurt me. Turn my sorrow to joy. And my trials to testimony. Instead of failure, give me success. Convert my shame to glory and my disgrace to honor.

- I cancel with the blood of Jesus, every evil vow, prophecy, and pronouncement against my life and destiny, in the name of Jesus(Numbers 23:23).

- Father, let Your Word preserve my life from dangers. Redirect me away from danger instead of hidden treasures. By Your Word, let me find my ways in this journey of life. Let Your Word guide me so that I will not be a victim of spiritual assassination or destruction in the mighty name of Jesus.

PRAYER STARTERS

- Father, armed me than aimed me in the right direction, show me how to fight; protect me with salvation armor; hold me up with a firm hand, that I may destroy the band of spiritual marauders, in Jesus' name (Psalm 144:1-2)

- Father, rescue me from squabbling people; make me a leader of nations. Ransom me from enemy's anger, pull me from the grip of upstarts, save my destiny from spiritual bullies (Psalm 18:43-45)

- Father, for thank You for my redemption through the blood of Jesus, I plead the blood of Jesus (for detoxification) I apply the blood of Jesus over every animate and inanimate object in my residence. The environment (For clearance) I soak myself in the blood of Jesus (For covering), I cover the doorpost of my house with the blood of Jesus (For protection)

- Father, arise for my defense and that of my family, my ministry, my business and Your church (Isaiah 37:33 -35)

- Father, establish and keep my life, home, and ministry from evil in the mighty name of Jesus. Praise be unto Your name! (2 Thessalonians 3:3; Deuteronomy 33:27)

PROTECT YOUR BRAND

Guard your secrets (Proverbs 21:23)

Have a password to your life (Micah 7: 5)

Avoid too much familiarity with people, especially new people.

Guard your heart against pollution and contamination
(Proverbs 4: 23; Philippians 4: 8)

Pay attention to your body 1 Corinthians 10:31; Proverbs 25: 27; 1
Corinthians 6:12; Romans 12: 1 ; Ecclesiastes 3: 13 ; 1 Corinthians
  6 :9)

Pay attention to your soul (Deuteronomy 4:29; Matthew 16:26;
 Psalm 42:11; 62 :1 ; Jeremiah 6 :16 ; 3 John 1:2 ; Psalm 139 : 13 -14 ;
Psalm 16:24

Pay attention to your spirit (Job 32:8; Proverbs 20:27; Romans
8:16 ; 1 Thessalonians 5:23 ;

Mind whom you associate with and know how to manage your
relationships (1 Corinthians 15:33; Psalm 26: 4;1 Thessalonians 5:22;
Psalm 1:1; 119:15; Proverbs 13:20; 14 :7; ; 20 :19; Jeremiah 51:6; Hosea
4:17

BOOKS BY
DAMOLA TREASURE OKENLA

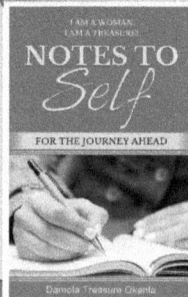

Books available on <u>AMAZON.COM</u>

Find us on social!

FACEBOOK

https://www.facebook.com/iamatreasuredwoman/

PINTEREST

https://www.pinterest.com/treasuredwoman1/

INSTAGRAM

https://www.instagram.com/iamatreasuredwoman/

Contact Us

 +1708-540-3090

 treasuredwoman1@gmail.com

 www.iamatreasuredwoman.com

ABOUT DAMOLA

As an award-winning author of several Christian books and a highly sought-after inspirational speaker, Damola Treasure Okenla is dedicated to uplifting others mentally, spiritually and emotionally. For more than ten years, she has partnered with individuals and groups to inspire and motivate others to live the life God intended for them to live—assisting them in rebuilding and recovering from losses and setbacks in life. As the president and founder of Life Encounters, Inc., a non-profit organization that is dedicated to self-discovery and recovery, Damola facilitates seminars, workshops and retreats to usher others into purpose fulfillment. Her organization, like her books, is a small reflection of her passion and mission for the advocacy of spiritual freedom and empowerment.

Damola serves as the president and founder of Hilltop Publishing, where she assists Christian authors with publishing and social media management for their book projects—positioning them for excellence in the marketplace. Apart from ministry, Damola works as an accountant and project manager, and holds a Master's in Public Administration. More than anything, Damola is on a mission to help others discover their true potential, live a life of purpose, and earn a profit while doing it.

For more information or bookings, visit www.damolatreasureokenla.com or call 800.767.0728.

ABOUT THE BOOK

I AM A WOMAN. I AM A TREASURE!
I AM COVERED.

In this easy - to- read book, you will find 31 Days - declarations and devotional prompters for meditation and inspiration to experience the supernatural security and satisfaction that flows from living under cover of the Almighty God. It is better to run from problems and people into the saving arms of God; for it is written, "God 's name is a place of protection- good people can run there and be safe." (Proverbs 18:10 MSG)God is our shelter and strength, always ready to help in times of trouble (Psalm 46:1 GNT). Hagar was a woman used, dumped, and deprived, but God met her at the point of need. God sees your need. The widow of Zarephath was at her lowest point, but God came through for her without her solicitation. Help is coming your way. A one chance encounter with Jesus turned a messed up woman to a divine messenger. Jesus rescued the Woman accused of adultery and condemned to death. Dear Woman, no matter what you are going through, no matter where you are, God's got you covered!
No matter the storm. Strength and dignity are your clothing; your position is stable and secure. You are a woman. You are a treasure! Rejoice for your future is bright, beautiful, and blessed!

On A Final Note!

The Lord is my best friend and my shepherd. I always have more than enough. He offers a resting place for me in his luxurious love.

His tracks take me to an oasis of peace, the quiet brook of bliss . That's where he restores and revives my life.

He opens before me pathways to God's pleasure and leads me along in his footsteps of righteousness so that I can bring honor to his name.

Lord, even when your path takes me through the valley of deepest darkness, fear will never conquer me, for you already have!

You remain close to me and lead me through it all the way. Your authority is my strength and my peace.

The comfort of your love takes away my fear. I'll never be lonely, for you are near . You become my delicious feast even when my enemies dare to fight.

You anoint me with the fragrance of your Holy Spirit; you give me all I can drink of you until my heart overflows. So why would I fear the future?

For your goodness and love pursue me all the days of my life.

Then afterward, when my life is through, I'll return to your glorious presence to be forever with you!

Psalms 23:1-6 TPT

www.ingramcontent.com/pod-product-compliance
Lightning Source LLC
Chambersburg PA
CBHW060533030426
42337CB00021B/4241